# How to Deal with ADHD in Teens

*Step by Step Guide on How to Successfully Deal with ADD and ADHD in Teens*

# Introduction

Lack of concentration can certainly affect performance at work, interactions and communication with others, and general well-being. Imagine someone going through this turmoil constantly. If you are a parent of a teen struggling with ADHD or are a teenager battling the same, you can understand the plight associated with the scenario.

ADHD can be quite perturbing and take a toll on your life if not handled with care and diligence. Unfortunately, there are not many comprehensive guides and literature on handling ADHD in teens.

Since adolescence comes with many changes, many perceived as hormonal changes, ADHD in adolescence is very easy to ignore. Only by understanding the issue can you tackle it successfully.

This book will give you insight into ADHD in teens and offers actionable and potent guidelines on managing it well. By the time you turn the last page, you will have learned enough to be in a position to tackle the issue well or provide assistance to your teenager kids, friends, and loved ones in taking care of their ADHD and living a better life.

PS: I'd like your feedback. If you are happy with this book, please leave a review on Amazon.

Please leave a review for this book on Amazon by visiting the page below:

https://amzn.to/2VMR5qr

# Table of Contents

**Introduction**............................................ **2**

**Chapter 1: Understanding ADHD in Teens .. 8**

Inability or lack of focus ................................. 10

Disorganized Behavior.................................... 11

Self-Focused ...................................................12

Fidgeting.........................................................13

Heightened Emotions .....................................13

Impulsivity......................................................15

Lack of Social Awareness................................15

**Chapter 2: Learn To Regulate Your Behavior**
................................................................**17**

Self-Regulation Skill ....................................... 18

Time-Management Skill ...................................19

Build a Routine ...............................................21

Explore Yourself .................................... 21

Surround Yourself with Positive People ............. 23

**Chapter 3: CBT Strategies to Combat ADHD**
**..................................................... 26**

Cognitive Behavioral Therapy (CBT) ................ 27

Journaling ........................................ 29

Identifying Patterns ............................ 29

Finding Solutions .............................. 31

Calm Down the Self-Doubt ....................... 31

Maintain Focus ................................ 32

**Chapter 4: Cognitive Restructuring and**
**Setting SMART Goals ............................... 34**

Cognitive Restructuring ........................... 34

Overgeneralizing ............................... 35

Catastrophizing ................................ 36

Mind Reading ................................................... 36

SMART Goals .................................................... 39

**Chapter 5: Try FORD and ECHO Strategies 42**

Use FORD ........................................................ 42

Family ............................................................ 43

Occupation ...................................................... 44

Recreation ....................................................... 45

Dreams ........................................................... 46

ECHO ............................................................. 48

**Chapter 6: Live in the Moment to Manage ADHD ............................................................. 52**

How Lack of Mindfulness Aggravates ADHD ..... 52

Avoid Distractions ............................................ 54

Practice Meditation to Inculcate Mindfulness .... 58

Ask for Help ..................................................... 62

# Chapter 7: Lifestyle Strategies—ADHD & Diet

..................................................... 65

Eat A Balanced Diet................................... 65

Eat Nutritious Food................................... 66

Supplementation Diets............................... 67

What You Should Not Eat ........................... 68

General Diet Tips for Teens with ADHD............. 71

Play Any Sport You Enjoy ........................... 74

Run Around the Block................................. 75

Do Some Stretches and Aerobics ................... 76

Start Small............................................. 76

Get Enough Shuteye.................................. 79

# Conclusion ............................................. 82

# Chapter 1: Understanding ADHD in Teens

Attention Deficit Hyperactive Disorder, generally called ADHD, is one of the most widespread neurodevelopmental disorders in children.[1] ADHD affects the functioning of your brain, consequently influencing your attention span and behavior.

In most cases, ADHD is identified in early childhood. However, there are cases where ADHD may be diagnosed later in life. According to a survey conducted by the Centers for Disease Control and Prevention in 2016, ADHD has been diagnosed in over 3.3 million children aged between 12 and 17 years.[2] Teenagers experiencing ADHD can find themselves struggling with everyday routines. They are also more prone to facing academic, social, or relationship issues.

It is essential to note that ADHD is different for different teenagers. Symptoms also differ across genders, by the situation or environment, individuals' personality, type of ADHD, or other disorders they may have. Children with

---

[1] https://www.psychiatry.org/patients-families/adhd/what-is-adhd
[2] https://www.cdc.gov/ncbddd/adhd/data.html

ADHD may also have additional conditions ranging from mental and behavioral to emotional.

The National Parent Survey of 2016 revealed that 64% of children suffering from ADHD also suffered from another mental, behavioral, or emotional disorder. Even though some ADHD symptoms are identifiable in the early years of a child's life, these symptoms are also observable in teenage years and adulthood.

Symptoms of ADHD can generally fall into three categories: hyperactivity, inattentiveness, or both[3]. There are cases where people fall in both or one of these categories.

- **ADHD Combined:** The most common type of ADHD presents both hyperactivity and distractibility symptoms.

- **Predominately Impulsivity-Hyperactivity:** This type of ADHD is the least common one of all these, and children suffering from this show impulsive behavior such as fidgeting, taking risks, interrupting, etc.

---

[3] https://www.cdc.gov/ncbddd/adhd/facts.html

- **Predominately Inattentive:** This is also known as Attention Deficit Disorder (ADD). The most predominant symptoms of this type are a child's inability to focus on a task, poor organizational skills, and getting distracted easily.

Below are symptoms commonly seen in teens suffering from ADHD:

### *Inability or lack of focus*

Teenagers have to juggle multiple tasks as their academic and social responsibilities increase. However, teens suffering from ADHD have problems completing one task or sticking to a single job. They may start one project only to start another in the middle of the first one. This normally causes them not to complete either duty. Their inability to focus can also cause them to make negligent errors while performing the task.

If you are a teen reading this, you would understand the scenario. All the times when you could not concentrate on a lecture in your school and kept drifting off in thought, even though you wanted to listen to the professor, and all the times when you would stop finding your routine PS games exciting are examples of this.

Due to lack of attention, teens suffering from ADHD are likelier to procrastinate. They may put off tasks, especially tasks that require a long time commitment, until close to the deadline. This can adversely affect their academic performance.

Those instances you knew you would not manage to study for your exam because you would struggle to concentrate and when you would not go to a baseball game because you knew you would get bored 10 minutes into the game are examples of times when ADHD triggers the urge to procrastinate.

## *Disorganized Behavior*

Teens with ADHD can often appear to lead unsystematic lives. Because of their lack of attention, they usually forget where they put things. It's understandable to misplace your car keys or wallet sometimes, but for children with ADHD, this is a routine issue. This can also lead them to be late for school and miss deadlines and appointments.

If you are a parent reading this, there must have been times when your teen would forget where he placed his baseball bat, or your teenage daughter would have a bad mood day just because she could not find her favorite skirt even though you reminded her several times to put it in the closet.

If you are a teen reading this, think of the times your parents and teachers in school chastised you for being irresponsible just because you kept missing your stuff. Yes, I know that pain because I once struggled with ADHD.

## *Self-Focused*

Children with ADHD can often get lost in their minds. They may be too focused on themselves, and it is often difficult for them to recognize other people's wants and wishes. They can miss social cues that are otherwise common to spot. Children suffering from ADHD may become too lost in their little world to wait for their turn. Thus, they can often be seen daydreaming or zoned out in class.

For teens reading this and struggling with ADHD, think of the instances when people called you self-absorbed and lost in your fantasies. Since you struggle to concentrate on one thing, it naturally feels easier to get lost in your world.

## *Fidgeting*

Squirming or restlessness is another symptom common among teens with ADHD because hyperactivity is a part of ADHD. These children will appear on edge in class, usually bouncing their legs anxiously, clicking the pen repeatedly, or always wiggling in their seats.

Have your parents, relatives, teachers, and other people ever called you 'annoying,' 'irritating,' 'restless,' or hyper? Your tendency to move around constantly and not stay fixed in a spot may be annoying to others. On the other hand, you know what a struggle it is for you.

## *Heightened Emotions*

Adolescents go through many life-changing experiences. Teen years are an emotional roller-coaster for anyone. However, they impact those suffering from ADHD more. According to a paper published in the Journal of Psychology & Psychotherapy,[4] children with ADHD reach emotional maturity later than their peers not suffering from ADHD.

---

4     https://www.longdom.org/open-access/emotional-maturity-and-adjustment-in-adhd-children-2161-0487.1000114.pdf

Thus, teens with ADHD are more susceptible to inappropriate emotional outbursts.

There would hardly be a kid who wouldn't go through an intense emotional phase in their adolescent years. Each one of us has been through that phase. It is hard!

Imagine how your teen who is already going through ADHD would feel right when puberty hits hard. It is certainly tough. Often, the dilemma is that neither your kid nor you are aware of the happening shift. Since you don't realize it is ADHD, and neither are they conscious of the issue, every emotional meltdown or reaction they show becomes labeled as adolescence kicking in or adolescent rebellion/hormones.

When your kid often shows intense emotional reactions to even petty situations, please take it as a sign of something bigger and take it seriously.

Similarly, if you are a teen reading this and want to be happy in life, observe your emotions closely. If you ever find yourself reacting too violently, or feeling immensely sad for no apparent reason, be courageous to discuss it with your parent.

While this book is right here by your side to guide you in the process and help you manage your ADHD, talking to your parents or guardians can make all the difference in the world.

## *Impulsivity*

Teens are more reckless than adults. However, those suffering from ADHD can make potentially dangerous and irresponsible decisions more quickly.

Although teens with ADHD are generally less hyperactive than their child counterparts, this is not without exception. Some teens can be involved in everything going on around them. You may leave them in the kitchen one minute, and the next, you may see them in their room engrossed in a video game.

## *Lack of Social Awareness*

ADHD also affects a teen's social skills. This can include the ability to hold and carry on conversations. Teens with ADHD cannot focus on conversations since they often get lost in their world or talk too much and interrupt the other person. They may do things like highjacking the conversation or leaving mid-discussion. They may also be unaware of when they have offended someone. This can negatively affect their social life and their ability to make friends.

ADHD is a combination of symptoms that can vary over time. Thus, ADHD can change as a child grows. Younger children are more prone to show hyperactivity than teens with ADHD.[5]

With the basics covered, let us discuss the different strategies and techniques you can employ to deal with ADHD in teens.

---

[5] https://childmind.org/article/adhd-in-teenagers/

# Chapter 2: Learn To Regulate Your Behavior

The last chapter looked at ADHD and its symptoms.

From this chapter, we shall seek to answer the most important question: successful ways of dealing with ADHD to minimize the associated risks and behavioral problems.

Though its effects vary from person to person, some common troubles teens experience are lack of focus, difficulty staying organized, and doing things in a hurry.

If you are a teen battling ADHD, there must have been times when you felt frustrated and misunderstood. Those feelings may have affected your relationships with friends and family and hindered your performance in school or college.

That said, you cannot let this hold you back. Learning techniques and strategies to build a coping mechanism is essential. Though it will take time, you will slowly learn to manage ADHD and train yourself to manage teenage attention deficit hyperactivity disorder (ADHD) by regulating your personality and behavior.

This chapter will discuss various strategies that teach you to take responsibility for your behavior without becoming dependent on others in your teen years.

## Self-Regulation Skill

A key skill that can help with dealing with ADHD is self-regulation. Self-regulation is your ability to observe your internal condition and adjust accordingly.

For example, you may experience difficulty explaining your point of view to your parent in an unusual situation. When you don't understand yourself well and cannot regulate your thoughts, emotions, and behavior, you may react to different things.

To avoid such situations, keep a check on yourself and train yourself to regulate your behavior. Here's what you can do:

- Set reminders on your phone every 2 hours to tune into your thoughts and behavior.

- When the alarm beeps, sit somewhere quiet and peaceful and think about your feelings.

- When you experience an urge to overreact, take stock of your emotions.

- Take deep breaths: inhale through your nose and exhale through your mouth.

- You can even lie down to take a rest momentarily.

- If you feel like it, stretch your arms and legs.

- Give yourself a break from what you are experiencing to have better control over your behavior.

- Work on yourself in this manner, excusing yourself from intense situations to practice self-regulation. Soon, you will get the hang of it and manage ADHD better.

Self-regulation comes with genuine intention and regular practice. If you are a parent of a teen struggling with ADHD, work with him/her to gradually teach him/her self-regulation.

## Time-Management Skill

Many teens with ADHD struggle to structure time because they cannot precisely recognize the flow of time. This is a lifelong problem, but you can work on this by developing time management skills. Developing better time management skills usually involves the following four steps:

- **Plan:** Learn to list and record all your daily activities in a paper or electronic planner. Think of all the tasks you wish to achieve beforehand, and put them on the planner. Keep the planner updated by marking completed tasks.

- **Prioritize:** You can prioritize your tasks by dividing them into two groups: important and unimportant, and always start by working on the important tasks, then move on to unimportant ones. A simple strategy is to pick the three most important tasks according to deadlines. Identify the three top important tasks, and tend to them first.

- **Schedule:** Record the estimated time and actual time to complete a task in your planner. By comparing the two, you can improve your time estimation and task efficiency.

- **Follow the plan:** The last and most important step in this sequence is religiously following the plan because planning without execution is a failure-bound exercise. You can display post-its with your to-do lists in a prominent place to remind you. You can also use smartphones apps to set reminders and timers.

## Build a Routine

Routines create discipline. You can build a consistent routine by performing your daily rituals at the same time each day. For example, getting up at the same time every day will help you establish a morning routine. Your morning routine can then include: waking up, going for a walk, showering, getting ready, having breakfast, taking your school bus every day, and following this pattern in the same order.

Similarly, you can establish an afternoon routine by doing the different things you plan on doing when you return home. Make sure to turn off your phone while doing homework to reduce disturbances. Ensure you have breaks in your daily schedule to avoid overwhelming yourself.

Use this approach to create a series of different routines in your life. You could have morning, noon, afternoon, evening, and nighttime routines you could adhere to religiously. Having routines will make it easier to stick to a schedule and streamline your life.

## Explore Yourself

Remember that having ADHD is just a part of you, not the whole you. There is a lot more to who you are that you must know and acknowledge. Explore your hidden talents and know your strengths. Maybe you are good at a particular sport, art, or technology. Your talent can be singing, dancing, cooking, or building things.

Here's what you should do:

- Spend some time reflecting on your talents, potentials, virtues, passions, and interests.

- Think of what you are good at, what you enjoy doing, what brings you joy, and the likes.

- Write down all the answers you get.

- Appreciate yourself for all the qualities you have. Say, "I feel good about being humble and caring."

- At the same time, make time for your interests and what you love doing. If you enjoy cycling, dedicate 10 to 15 minutes of your day to cycling around the block. Similarly, if listening to rock music calms you down, carve out time for that.

Once you start exploring yourself and doing things that spark joy, you will feel good about yourself.

# Surround Yourself with Positive People

*"You are the average of the five people you spend the most time with."*

### *Jim Rohn*

We often think that our behavior only depends on our thoughts and actions. The truth is that the people around us also affect our behavior and actions. If you hang out with people who trigger your insecurities, make fun of you, pull you down, and are unkind to you, you will naturally feel disturbed, which may set off your ADHD.

Your goal should be to surround yourself with people who see you for who you are, not what you lack. By spending time with positive, uplifting, and compassionate people, you will feel comforted and good about yourself. As a result, you would find it easy to regulate yourself and your behavior.

Here's what you need to start doing more:

- Closely observe the people you hang out with the most, including your friends, neighbors, family members, etc.

- Pay attention to how different people make you feel. Perhaps you are in a reading club, and one of the members has a bad habit of picking on everyone. Maybe he/she says mean things that put you off and trigger your ADHD.

- Once you figure out who those people are in your social circle, start distancing yourself from them. You can do that by avoiding their calls, not replying to their messages, talking less with them, and taking a route to school that minimizes your interaction with such people.

- At the same time, identify the positive influences in your circle, and start spending time with them. These are all the people who give off positive vibes and make you feel good about yourself.

- For the parents of ADHD teens, start talking more to your kids without being too intrusive. Instead of asking too many questions about who they spend time with, take an interest in their activities. Gradually, they will open up to you and fill you in with details that can help you guide them about positive and negative influences accordingly.

It takes time to fine-tune your social circle or that of your kids. But with consistent effort, it will happen with time, and you will start observing great results in your mood, behavior, and ADHD tendencies.

Let us move to the next chapter and discuss some social strategies to help teens deal with ADHD.

# Chapter 3: CBT Strategies to Combat ADHD

Living with ADHD can prove challenging for anyone, especially teenagers. Experiencing ADHD makes life difficult on many levels, including the social life level.

You are likely to struggle with socializing with people, interacting with other kids in school, speaking confidently in front of others, particularly in a class lecture, and saying what you feel.

Perhaps, you have a crush on someone at school but find it nearly impossible to approach the person. You probably feel like participating in the drama club but cannot bring yourself to recite the dialogues and mingle with other participants because you keep feeling distracted.

Many experts believe that when it comes to treating symptoms of ADHD in teens, medication is often not necessary. A lot of the time, behavioral therapy and a strong support system are enough to manage symptoms. So, the question that comes to mind is, "How is that possible?"

Let's answer that question together.

CBT, aka Cognitive Behavioral Therapy, is a powerful set of strategies that can help you slowly gain better control of your condition. Let us discuss it in detail in this chapter.

## Cognitive Behavioral Therapy (CBT)

Many psychologists consider Cognitive Behavioral Therapy a golden standard of psychotherapy.[6] Due to its importance, we will discuss this strategy in detail. Furthermore, we will explain different ways of incorporating this strategy into your daily routine, thereby making your life easier.

Let's answer the question that has probably been on your mind, "What is Cognitive Behavioral Therapy?"

CBT is an umbrella term for various techniques that can help you identify and change unhealthy behavioral patterns. According to the American Psychological Association, the core notion of CBT revolves around three things:

- Negative thinking is partially responsible for psychological problems.

---

[6] https://www.ncbi.nlm.nih.gov/pmc/articles/PMC5797481/

- Unhealthy learned behavior is to some extent responsible for psychological problems.

- People who are suffering from psychological problems can relieve their symptoms by learning more effective coping mechanisms.

I am sure you want to know how this technique can be useful in social settings. The answer is that it's helpful in multiple ways. It can help teens with ADHD by:

- Improving their perception of other people's thinking processes.

- Identifying how to react in otherwise problematic situations

- Learning how to face challenges

- Effectively using calming techniques

- Using role-play to disarm possibly sticky situations.

Now that we have established its usefulness and relevance, let's move on to the practical implementation. One of the ways to implement Cognitive Behavioral Therapy is through:

# Journaling

At first glance, you might be surprised and think this strategy is impossible to implement. After all, journaling involves everything that is normally hard for people with ADHD to do, such as sitting for long periods while focusing on writing and avoiding distractions.

That is precisely why it is so helpful for teenagers with ADHD. It allows you to slow down, gather your thoughts, process your emotions, and improve your mood.

Some of the ways journaling can help you in your daily routine are by:

## *Identifying Patterns*

Forgetfulness is one of the main challenges people with ADHD face. They are easily distracted by everything going on in their life that they struggle to track details.

When you write everything down, you can look back and identify major themes or patterns causing delays or problems. For instance, how many times have you had to buy new stationery because you misplaced your old one or missed the party or maybe you keep forgetting to take your reading material to school?

## **Solution:**

- Before going to bed, write everything that happened during the day. No matter how small an activity seems, jot it down.

- Record everything from how you felt to what you did.

- The next morning, go over what you wrote. Reflect on your routine, and try to analyze it objectively —this will help you develop a better understanding of how you function.

- Do this consistently for a week.

- After some time, you will start seeing patterns and themes.

- Identify the harmful ones and try to overcome them. Perhaps, you go to your school on foot with a neighbor who tends to talk about things that somehow trigger your ADHD. Once you journal and analyze your routine for a week, you may realize how that little act of walking to school with that friend upsets you.

- Once you figure out the patterns, change your routine and life accordingly.

## *Finding Solutions*

Journaling is also a great way to answer any questions you might have. Suppose you want to know what you can do to make friends with a certain person in school. Ask the journal. No, I am not kidding. It will give you the answer. People with ADHD tend to be very creative. What this technique does is give you creative solutions to those problems.

- In the journal, ask any questions you have. For example, "How can I ask Adam to be my friend?"

- Then below that question, think of different ways to accomplish that task.

This will allow you to think ahead and pre-plan your social interactions, which will ensure you don't get caught completely off-guard. You will also feel less anxious.

## *Calm Down the Self-Doubt*

Teens with ADHD often find themselves trapped in uncertainty. They question their ability to perform specific tasks as well as their peers.

For instance, in a situation, you may think, "I can't do this." Turn this into a positive thought, maybe something like, "I just need to find a new and creative way to complete my task."

However, at times, merely thinking is not enough. It helps to have some confirmation, which is where journaling comes in.

- Keep a paper and pen —a notebook is better— on you at all times.

- On a page in the journal, draw a vertical line in the center.

- Whenever you notice a negative thought, note it down.

- On the other side of the line, write a positive thought.

- Read that positive thought out loud.

- Keep reading it until you believe it.

## *Maintain Focus*

The impulsivity that often comes with ADHD makes it challenging for teens to stick to a single task. You may often get distracted when talking to a friend or leave your homework incomplete to do something you just remembered. That happens, and it is okay. Let's see a trick that can help you maintain focus.

- Each time you are sitting down to work, keep your journal by your side.

- When you remember something you need to do, open your journal and note down the task instead of getting up to do it.

- Tell yourself you will do it after you have completed this one.

- Review your journal at the end of the day. You will find that most of the tasks that seemed important then weren't.

Those were some ways journaling can help deal with ADHD in social settings. In addition, there are more social strategies under the umbrella of CBT that work magically in calming down ADHD in teens.

Let's discuss them in the following chapter.

# Chapter 4: Cognitive Restructuring and Setting SMART Goals

This chapter will explore another useful technique that falls under Cognitive Behavioral Therapy. Some people even call this technique the backbone of CBT.

## Cognitive Restructuring

Do not worry! Cognitive restructuring is not as scary as it sounds—quite the opposite. Put plainly:

Cognitive restructuring means changing the way you think to reach a positive conclusion.

Yes!

In this chapter, we will be learning that everything is rainbows and cupcakes, and you will find gold at the end of the rainbow.

It is fairly easy to think of the worst-case scenario when in various situations; however, these scenarios are seldom the reality.

There are situations where things seem black and white. But that is mostly not the case. Instead of jumping to conclusions and catastrophizing the situation, help your teens struggling with ADHD understand the situation from a different point of view. Support them to see a different perspective.

Go about things pragmatically instead of jumping to the worst possible scenario. It is not that difficult to put a different spin on things. All you need to do is question the possibility and think of what more a situation has to offer.

If your teen feels he/she is terrible at something and shares the concern with you, don't shun it. Instead, motivate your teen to think about where the feeling comes from and why they feel that way. Then, help your teen son or daughter go through his or her strengths and acknowledge them.

Let us take a deeper look at cognitive restructuring and what it tackles. Cognitive restructuring helps to deal with three types of negative thoughts.

## *Overgeneralizing*

This refers to overgeneralizing any situation. Due to the impulsive behavior of teens with ADHD, they jump to conclusions faster than you can say, "Let us think about it."

For example, imagine you failed to secure good marks on a test. You would overgeneralize the situation into something like, "I can't do anything right," Or "I will never succeed in life."

## Catastrophizing

Bad things happen to everyone. However, the tendency of teens with ADHD to exaggerate the negative impact is not helpful for themselves or anyone else.

For example, you may have forgotten to wish your friend a happy birthday and now think that your friend will never g talk to you again. That is not the case. Just apologize, and everything will be alright.

Similarly, if you are a parent to a teen, you may have heard your son or daughter saying how the slightest change in events ruined his or her day.

## Mind Reading

Impulsivity is a big part of ADHD, and it is especially tricky to handle social situations when you are reckless. Teens with ADHD often make mistakes and then assume that people now hate them.

For instance, you interrupted someone while they were speaking, and now you think they consider you pesky and irritating.

Let's see how you can shift these negative thoughts into more realistic and positive ones.

For this purpose, I will help you build a structured framework you can follow for every situation.

This framework will consist of 7 steps:

1. Identify the situation

2. Note your thoughts

3. Understand your emotions and feelings,

4. Gather evidence that supports your thoughts

5. Collect information that does not line up with your thoughts

6. Identify a balanced thought.

7. Ask yourself, "How do I feel now?"

Now let me explain this process with a scenario.

**Situation:** Suppose you found out that two of your friends went to the movies and did not invite you.

**Thought:** "My friends dislike me. They think I am bothersome. That is why they went without me."

**Emotions:** Sad, lonely, and possibly angry.

**Evidence supporting the thought**: "I talked over one of them today/I argued with them the other day."

**Evidence against the thought:** "They invite me to hang out, and they have told me they consider me a good friend."

**Reasonable thought:** "My friends have their own lives, and it is unfair to expect them to make me a part of everything. Just because they did not invite me once doesn't mean they don't like me."

**How do I feel now?** Unbothered and peaceful

Practice cognitive restructuring with your thoughts in this manner every time you feel disturbed or bombarded by a barrage of upsetting thoughts. Journaling will come in very handy here. Journal your thoughts so you can track them and your progress. Soon, you will be in better control of how you think, feel, and behave.

While working on this strategy, start setting SMART goals.

## SMART Goals

Teens suffering from ADHD are easily distracted. Big projects often seem daunting, and because they often fail to complete them, they suffer academically.

An effective way to counter this is to break big projects into smaller, more manageable tasks. The SMART Goals approach is the best way to do this. SMART stands for **s**pecific, **m**easurable, **a**chievable, **r**ealistic, and **t**imed/**t**ime-bound.

If you have a project, break that into goals that are:

- **Specific:** Set a goal with a clear attainment point rather than something vague like success. For example, instead of saying, "I will do well this year." Say, "I will study every day for two hours to help myself secure an A in my final exams."

- **Measurable:** Have a proper metric against which you can gauge your progress towards the goal. Don't say, "I need to finish reading this book." Instead, say, "I will complete this book by the end of the week."

- **Achievable:** Base your goals on your capability to ensure you don't set the bar too high or low. Be kind and gentle with yourself, try to exceed your limits, but at the same time, remember you are human, and there is only so much you can do.

- **Realistic:** Unrealistic goals set all the other metrics of SMART goals out of order: it works against the SMART goal setting model. If you know that achieving the goals is impossible, you won't try to achieve them.

- **Timed:** Have a proper timeframe and deadline by which you want to have attained your goals. Every good project or goal has a start and end date. Make sure yours has one too.

Once you have identified your goal using the SMART approach, you need to think of proper steps you can take to bring that goal to fruition. An effective way to do this is with the acronym TAKE.

- **Think:** Actively think about ways to achieve your goals, and note down the steps you can take to accomplish your objective.

- **Actualize:** Genuinely start working towards the set goals now with the steps in mind. The first step is always the hardest, but you can do it.

- **Keep track:** Set milestones to track your progress towards your goal and do your best to avoid getting distracted. Can you remember the technique we discussed in the last chapter about noting down tasks that distract you from what you are doing at the moment, begging for your immediate attention? Utilize it here as well.

- **Evaluate:** Assess whether you are on track towards your goal. Often the first set goal isn't the final goal. Modify your goal as per your current progress.

These hacks are quite effective; you only need to be consistent with them, and as you practice them more, you'll notice a marked improvement in your concentration. Continue to build this momentum by working on the next set of strategies in the following chapter.

# Chapter 5: Try FORD and ECHO Strategies

A big challenge for teens with ADHD is difficulty or inability to hold conversations. This chapter will discuss some communication tips and tricks to help you have smooth and meaningful conversations.

These techniques are not just for teens with ADHD—anyone can use them. However, people that do not have ADHD tend to use these subconsciously rather than deliberately, especially teens. One reason for this is that teenagers have to deal with and meet several people in their daily lives, whether in school or at a party.

## Use FORD

While role-playing different scenarios might be helpful for younger children with ADHD, it is often not as effective for teenagers. Teens experience a wide variety of situations, and it is next to impossible to train them for every interaction they may have.

Due to this, teens with ADHD often find themselves unprepared and missing social cues or being at a loss for words. An easy and effective way to keep the ball rolling in a conversation is through a technique called FORD.

FORD stands for: family, occupation, recreation, and dreams. Asking about one or all of these could help keep the conversation going smoothly.

On the plus side, these topics are highly unlikely to offend anyone, and people almost always have something to say about them and are open to discussing such topics.

Let's see how you can put this handy method to good use.

## *Family*

Possible questions could be:

- How many siblings do you have?

- What do your parents do?

- How is your bond with your siblings?

- Do you get to see your cousins often?

- Do you have family dinners?

You can take these questions and build on them with other related ones. For instance, once you ask about someone's siblings, you can further ask what they do, their likes, passions, etc. If you are talking about family dinners, talk about the meals they share, their favorite foods, restaurants they have been to, and other such question.

Take every question as an opportunity to dig more into a conversation and gradually grow it. It takes some time to get the hang of it, but you will do it if you stay consistent.

### *Occupation*

Some conversation starters may be:

- How are your studies going?

- Do you have a part-time job?

- What is your favorite subject?

- If you are working somewhere, what is your job like?

- Have you thought of some sort of internship?

- What subject do you not enjoy at all?

- How do you make your academics more enjoyable?

Similarly, keep exploring the different aspects of this category. Don't just stop at asking one question. Instead, wait for the response and then ask another question accordingly. If you asked someone about their studies, you could ask about their favorite subject.

## *Recreation*

You could try asking about:

- What are your hobbies?

- What do you do to relax?

- Do you prefer books or movies?

- What is your favorite adventure sport? Or do you enjoy adventure sports?

- What is a holiday destination you have always wanted to visit?

- What are the activities/tourist spots on your bucket list?

- What do you do for recreation and leisure?

Like with the other two aspects discussed above, don't stick to just these basic questions with this one. When asking someone about how they relax, talk about the activity they enjoy and the people they like to do those activities with.

If talking to someone about books or movies, talk about the genre of movies they watch and the kind of books they enjoy reading. Feel free to throw in your ideas too. You can talk about the things you enjoy doing. For example:

If you started cycling during the COVID-19 lockdown, you could talk about how it brought you relief and peace. If you have recently developed a liking for reading biopics, I know it may feel difficult at first, but give it a try, and you will feel just fine.

### *Dreams*

This one is my favorite because it gives you great insight into the other person—plus, who doesn't like talking about the endless possibilities the future might hold? For this question, I highly recommend you come up with questions that resonate with you, but some possible ones may be:

- If you could pick any career, what would it be?

- What is one place you have always wanted to visit?

- If you had three wishes, what would you wish for?

- What is your biggest and most genuine dream?

- Do you believe in dreams coming true?

- What do you feel your purpose in life is?

- What do you often dream about?

- Do you ever daydream? If yes, what is it about mostly?

** Here, "dream" refers to the dreams you see when asleep and symbolizes your wishes, wants, needs, desires, and aspirations. You can take this as an opportunity to know more about what the other person wants in life and their desires.

This technique can help you avoid uncomfortable silences and make it easier to know someone. However, you might want to refrain from asking questions that feel too personal or prying. The best practice is to ask something general and leave it to the other person to go as deep into it as they feel comfortable. Once they have responded, you could give your response to that question or ask a question you feel is relevant to their response.

Conversations may be somewhat awkward at first, but as you go on, you will notice a considerable improvement in your abilities to hold a conversation. Eventually, you will not need this trick to help your conversations flow. You will also be more aware of social norms and cues such as maintaining appropriate eye contact, finding appropriate moments to talk about various topics, paying attention to people as they talk, and not interrupting when someone else is speaking.

Moreover, this technique helps you feel more emotionally in tune with those around you. These questions are the first step to establishing deeper, more meaningful connections and relationships.

## ECHO

It is common for people with ADHD to be easily distracted and impulsive. Due to this, they often have their attention somewhere else, making them miss crucial information in their social interactions. This can cause confusion and miscommunication. It can also hurt the other person as they may think you are not interested in what they have to say.

To keep this from happening, use the ECHO technique. ECHO is what it sounds like: If you are not sure whether you heard something correctly or not, you could repeat or ECHO what you heard.

Most of us unintentionally do this when someone asks us a question. People do this as it gives them time to comprehend the question and develop appropriate answers.

For teenagers with ADHD, it is that much more valuable a tool. It helps them stay focused and minimizes the chances of communication errors that may have occurred due to inattentiveness, but it is also a subtle enough trick to not seem out of place in the conversation.

There are three different ways you can do this:

- Repeat the question or statement you think you heard word for word. If you heard the other person say, "Chemistry is quite hard and really tests my nerves at times." You could say the same. If you feel the other person may find it awkward seeing you repeat their sentence word to word, you could say it under your breath. For simple statements that state a fact or something routine, you can easily repeat them out loud.

- Or you could paraphrase it. For example, "So, what you mean to ask is …." If someone stated a personal preference or described a personal routine, you could rephrase it.

- Ask for clarification. Use statements like, "Can you please elaborate on what you meant?" For instance, if someone expressed their resentment about closing their business, ask them about their feelings. If someone said they don't like Van Gogh's art much, ask them why. You could probe into questions and ask others to express their sentiments fully. This helps keep the conversation going.

While the ways mentioned above are good for direct communication, teens with ADHD should also focus on non-verbal one. Try to guess what people are thinking through their gestures, facial expressions, and body language.

In the beginning, identify easier signals. For instance, before trying this on actual people, practice deciphering the emotions of movie characters. This will give you an idea of how people communicate non-verbally.

If you find it hard, try to pick out common cues such as sneering or rolling the eyes.

Social interactions play a significant role in the definitive years of teenagers, so it would not be a lie to say teens live and breathe social relations. Try implementing these techniques to find out which of the above technique resonates more with your personality and see the difference in your interactions with others.

Happy Socializing!

You need more than socializing strategies to have a better grip on ADHD. The next chapter highlights some powerful strategies that can help you with this task.

# Chapter 6: Live in the Moment to Manage ADHD

Teenagers with ADHD have distinctive learning requirements than children without ADHD. These teens can be immensely innovative and imaginative. However, ADHD symptoms such as distractibility, impulsivity, and hyperactivity, make it challenging for them to study with a similar approach or at an identical pace as their peers.

Such students often struggle to maintain focus, stay organized, and complete the assignments they began. Consequently, adolescents with ADHD need a little extra support to succeed in school.

## How Lack of Mindfulness Aggravates ADHD

ADHD strikes hard because of an inability to live in the moment. Unfortunately, many of us are in the habit of doing multiple things at a time and hanging on to multiple branches of thought simultaneously. This state of mind is also known as the 'monkey state of mind.' Like how a monkey leaps from one tree branch to another and is constantly moving, we tend to think of numerous things simultaneously.

Those struggling with ADHD go through an even harder time due to this state of mind. Naturally, when you are constantly wandering off in thought, you struggle more to focus on your current task. The perfect antidote to this issue is to cultivate a state of mindfulness.

You might be wondering what mindfulness is. Mindfulness means directing all your attention towards a task, an activity, or whatever you are doing right now. It refers to being completely consciously present in the moment and whatever it entails.

While doing so, you need to nurture a nonjudgmental, peaceful, and accepting attitude. With this attitude, you find it easy to embrace everything that comes with the moment. You feel more focused in the moment, which automatically helps you manage your ADHD.

However, in the beginning, you need to put in conscious effort to be mindful because you are new to the practice. I am sure you know how our habits function in autopilot mode, which means that once we build a habit of something, we engage in it without thinking much or putting in much effort.

Similarly, you have developed the habit of thinking about multiple things simultaneously and working on tasks with a distracted state of mind; this habit is now in your autopilot system, which is why it feels natural to operate in a distracted state. That is why it will take some time to work on tasks consciously and mindfully.

Once you build a habit of staying mindful, it will come to you naturally. However, people with ADHD often struggle to pay attention to the tasks and activities they need to perform, including conscious mindfulness.

How can teens with ADHD practice mindfulness?

This chapter will focus on various techniques you can practice to become more mindful and live in the moment. These approaches will gradually help you manage ADHD symptoms and find it easier to concentrate in class and shine in academics.

## *Avoid Distractions*

As previously discussed, students with ADHD can lose focus rapidly because of the symptoms associated with ADHD. For the first technique, we will see how we can mitigate these disruptions and help improve attention span.

What to do?

- Try working on one task at a time. Whatever you do, just tend to one activity at a time. For example, if you are reading a book, consciously fixate your attention on reading. Avoid tending to any other task at that time. This is an effective way of blocking out distractions to keep doing one thing engagingly.

- To be mindful in your studies, sit in the front of the class. This will help reduce distractions because it will lower the barriers between you and the instructor. Furthermore, there will be fewer distractions since other students will be behind you.

- When working on a task, be it reading your Physics book, creating a presentation, doing your shift at the restaurant, or even something fun such as playing your Xbox, put your phone on silent to ensure you don't get sidetracked by incoming notifications and messages. Mobile phones and gadgets are some of the biggest distractions —we spend an average of 6 to 7 hours on our phones. That's a whole lot of time! Imagine how much we can achieve in life if we devote those 6 hours to something worthwhile. Moreover, the blue rays emitted by screens mess up our concentration, sleep cycle, and ability to focus, leaving us feeling jittery and distracted. Start reducing your screen time by consciously putting your phone away when working on any task, even when cleaning the kitchen counter.

- Sit next to positive peer models who are more likely to focus on the lesson in class. Positive behaviors such as this tend to reflect on the people that sit next to them. When you surround yourself with focused people, your focus naturally improves.

- If you recall some other responsibilities you had to do, jot them down somewhere rather than doing them right away.

- Moreover, sit somewhere peaceful and calmly analyze all the different distractions you often give in to. What are the different temptations that lure you away from your work or important tasks? Do you often get calls from friends? Or do you spend hours taking pictures using Snapchat filters? Or are you glued to Whatsapp often? Or do you binge-watch movies on Netflix? Each one of us has some weaknesses to which we surrender. Find out what yours are, and then write them down.

Once you have analyzed your distractions, create a 'temptation management strategy plan' for each temptation. For instance, if you are addicted to Snapchat, you could set reminders not to use it, block the app, or gradually reduce how much time you spend on the app.

- Start working on these guidelines, and you will soon mindfully have a tighter grip on your distractions. As you block them better, you will find it easier to live in the moment and work on your tasks while managing ADHD symptoms.

What not to do?

- Don't sit near high distraction places such as doors and windows while working on an important task. Sitting close to openings and other places of the sort drives your attention towards things going on outside.

- Don't sit next to people who are loud and distracting. This could also include your friends. Sitting with them in class may divert your attention.

- Don't keep a question in your head. As soon as a query pops up in your head, attempt to ask the teacher immediately. Otherwise, the teacher will move to another point or topic, leaving your attention split between that and your question. Similarly, if you need to talk to someone, do it right away instead of letting that idea or thought sit in your head for long.

- Refrain from juggling many tasks simultaneously.

## Practice Meditation to Inculcate Mindfulness

Meditation is a beautiful and soothing practice that centers your attention on the here and now. Naturally, as you focus better on the moment, you become mindful of it. That's how meditation induces a state of mindfulness.

Moreover, meditation enhances attentiveness, concentration,[7] memory and decreases stress. It does this by helping clear your mind of disruptive, stressful, and chaotic thoughts. Naturally, when you have a de-cluttered mind, you feel relaxed and find it easy to focus on one task at a time. Learn to meditate by practicing it every day.

A simple meditation technique you can learn easily is the "7/11 breath" technique commonly used in high-pressure

---

[7] https://kidshealth.org/en/teens/adhd-tips.html

jobs such as police, firefighting, or teaching. Here is how you can practice it:

- First, breathe in for 7 seconds.

- While inhaling, do so through your nose.

- Watch your breath closely and calmly as you inhale.

- Next, breathe out for 11 seconds.

- Exhale through your mouth.

- Repeat it several times.

After a few repetitions, you will feel that your brain babble has calmed down reasonably and sense a physical peace. If you repeat the 7/11 breath 12-15 times, you will soon master 4 to 6 breaths per minute. This is an optimum range that's scientifically verified to achieve long-term focus.

You can also consult a psychologist who can teach you mindfulness techniques.

**NOTE:** Researchers are still researching how mindfulness raises self-awareness and builds self-control in teens with ADHD.

In addition, practice the following meditative technique to clear your head.

- Sit comfortably and pick what you want to pay attention to (something simple like your breathing).

- Focus on that alone; optionally, close your eyes to immerse yourself. Don't try to force it; rather, try to be aware of each breath.

- Take notice of when your mind wanders to other thoughts. When this happens, attempt to bring your concentration back to your breathing.

- Repeat this process for a few minutes every day to train your attention and be more mindful.

This was one example. You do not have to limit yourself to just meditative mindfulness. Try to implement this practice in all your activities.

For instance,

- Pay attention to your surroundings when traveling to school, or

- Be mindful of the taste of the food you are chewing, or

- Even the words you are speaking, focus on the vocabulary. Use words that relax you.

Now that we've covered what mindfulness is and you can practice it, keep trying to be consciously aware of what is happening and what you are doing until it becomes second nature.

Let's discuss what its advantages are.

Some benefits that aid the learning process are:

- Being deliberately alert of what is occurring in class

- Learning to suppress distractions

- Remaining composed in tense circumstances

- Having more self-control

- Completing the work you started

- Enjoying an activity you are performing

It is valuable to note that anybody can reap these benefits – including people with ADHD.

## *Ask for Help*

You are probably wondering how asking for help relates to living in the moment and inculcating a sense of mindfulness.

The truth is that nobody is strong enough to do everything or accomplish every task alone. When we cannot do something alone, we let our guilt and sometimes even shame wash us over. We feel upset, confused, disturbed, and stressed in those moments. That's when we drift off into thought somewhere in the past or future, but nowhere in the present. More upsetting thoughts loom over us, and we find it challenging to manage our emotions.

This particular struggle becomes even more challenging for those battling ADHD. If you ask for help when you need it, you will calm down and prevent the series of reactions that trigger your hyperactivity.

There is no shame in asking for help. If you believe you need a little extra support from your teachers, peers, friends, family, or anyone else, don't be reluctant to ask. Most of your teachers or the people around you would be aware of the symptoms of ADHD and can even provide valuable insight on how to deal with it better in your academic life. For those who aren't knowledgeable on the subject, I request the parents to step in and talk to the concerned people.

Since you'll be in school most of the time, let's discuss how you can build a better bond with your teachers and take their help to stay calm. Remember, your teachers are there to educate and guide you, not just deliver their lectures. Let your teachers help you!

- Talk with them and explain your disorder to ensure they know your situation better.

- Discuss things you like and things you don't. This can help them upgrade their lesson plans to match your needs.

- Talk about your hobbies and interests outside of the classroom. Is there a way they can incorporate those into their lessons?

- Explain your interests and what part of their teaching style you find challenging to follow. This will allow them to alter their teaching methods accordingly.

This conversation will help instructors create a tailored plan that would suit your education needs. For instance, the professor may give you assignments broken down into smaller tasks so you can do them more easily.

When they learn more about you, they may modify their teaching approach to accommodate your needs. Maybe, they could do that by designing a more interactive class atmosphere or using more visual diagrams to teach their course.

Moreover, if you have trouble sitting still for long periods, they could arrange in-class activities that permit you to move around.

Now that we've covered learning strategies, start applying them.

Happy learning!

Let us now move towards some helpful lifestyle strategies that too can do wonders in dealing with ADHD in teens.

# Chapter 7: Lifestyle Strategies—ADHD & Diet

Food and nutrition play an important role in maintaining the health of teens diagnosed with ADHD. Dietary changes have helped many deal with hyperactivity, lack of focus, and impulsivity.

Many teens with ADHD and their parents are willing to try an ADHD diet that helps manage symptoms, but they don't know where to start. This chapter will teach you a few strategies to adopt the healthiest foods for an ADHD brain.

## Eat A Balanced Diet

Research has shown that eating a balanced diet can help combat the symptoms of ADHD. You can live a healthier life by including fish, whole grains, fruits, and vegetables[8] in your daily diet.

Moreover, extensive research has discovered a positive relationship between omega-3s and ADHD. These are present in salmon, leafy green vegetables, walnuts, and

---

[8] https://www.webmd.com/food-recipes/ss/slideshow-exotic-fruits

flaxseeds. Eating a healthy diet will help your brain[9] function better and deal better with ADHD symptoms like impatience or lack of concentration.

## Eat Nutritious Food

According to expert opinion, eating nutritious food is good for your brain. Hence, teens with ADHD should include the following foods in their diet to fulfill overall nutrition needs:

- **A high-protein diet**. Foods rich in proteins include beans, dairy products (milk, cheese, and yogurt), poultry (eggs[10] & white meat), and nuts. You must add these foods to your breakfast and afternoon snacks. It can increase your focus and help ADHD medications work well.

- **More complex carbohydrates.** These are good for your health and are plentiful in vegetables and fruits such as kiwi, apples, grapefruit, pears and oranges.

---

[9] https://www.webmd.com/brain/picture-of-the-brain
[10] https://www.webmd.com/food-recipes/ss/slideshow-eggs-6-ways

Eating this kind of food in the evening will help you sleep[11] better.

- **More omega-3 fatty acids.** Scientific research has proven that foods rich in omega-3 fatty acids work against ADHD symptoms.[12] These are present in fishes like tuna, salmon, and cold-water white fish.[13] Other sources of omega-3 fatty acids are walnuts, Brazil nuts, olive oil, and canola oil.

## Supplementation Diets

If you don't get enough nutrition from your diet, consider taking food supplements, especially vitamins and minerals. These can make up for the deficiency of essential nutrients you must get to treat ADHD symptoms.

There is divided opinion among experts regarding the use of food supplements. Some suggest that it is 100% mandatory for people with ADHD to take a vitamin and mineral supplement each day. In some cases, experts recommend an omega-3 fatty acid supplement. Vayarin is an omega

---

[11] https://www.webmd.com/sleep-disorders/default.htm
[12] https://www.additudemag.com/adhd-diet-for-kids-food-fix/
[13] https://www.webmd.com/food-recipes/ss/slideshow-foolproof-fish

compound approved by the FDA as part of the ADHD management strategy.

Other nutrition experts believe that individuals who take a balanced diet do not require vitamins or other nutrient supplements. Not enough scientific evidence is available to support the notion that food supplements help out all the teens who have this disorder.

Teens must be careful in taking mega-doses of vitamins as they can be toxic. Since ADHD symptoms vary from person to person, it is better to consult your doctor before considering a supplementation diet.

## What You Should Not Eat

Some foods or ingredients can trigger certain behaviors or worsen ADHD symptoms. Thus, try to identify and eliminate any such food or ingredient from your diet. If it aggravates your condition, you should stay away from that food. Experts recommend that people with ADHD avoid the following foods:

- **Simple carbohydrates**. Many people don't know that our body digests and converts simple processed carbs into glucose. Hence, you should cut down on candies, corn syrup, honey, white bread, white rice, waffles, and potatoes without skin.

- **Food additives:**[14] Various studies propose that artificial additives such as food colors & preservatives amplify hyperactivity in teens struggling with ADHD. Foods high in artificial flavors include Gatorade, cheese puffs, colorful cereals, candies, and soft drinks. Try to replace these foods with fresh, unprocessed foods as they contain fewer or zero additives. You can also find additive-free foods such as bread, cereals, and cookies by carefully reading the labels and ingredients. Cheerios are better as they contain less sugar. Fresh fruit juices and fruit punches are much healthier than soft drinks.

- **Sugar:**[15] Some teens become over energetic after eating sugary foods. Though no research has identified sugar as a direct cause of ADHD, it is better to cut down on sugary foods because it can help maintain

---

[14]    https://www.webmd.com/diet/features/the-truth-about-seven-common-food-additives
[15] https://www.webmd.com/diet/rm-quiz-sugars-sweeteners

your health. You can also see if this improves your symptoms.

- <u>**Caffeine**</u>:[16] It may surprise you that a small amount of caffeine can help with <u>ADHD symptoms</u>[17] in some cases. However, the side effects of <u>caffeine</u>[18] outweigh its potential benefits. Hence, it is better to avoid taking <u>caffeine</u>[19]—in any form—as it can interfere with ADHD medication.

- **Allergens.** Some researchers suggest that eliminating potential allergens from your food can develop better focus and decrease hyperactivity. However, this can only benefit those who have any actual intolerance to wheat, soy, or gluten. You must discuss food allergies with your dietician to avoid any mishaps.

---

[16] https://www.webmd.com/diet/caffeine-myths-and-facts
[17] https://www.webmd.com/add-adhd/adhd-health-check/default.htm
[18] https://www.webmd.com/sleep-disorders/video/breus-caffeine-insomnia
[19] https://www.webmd.com/diet/rm-quiz-caffeine-myths

## General Diet Tips for Teens with ADHD

We suggest following general diet tips that benefit teens with ADHD:

- Eat a balanced diet by including various foods such as vegetables, fruits, whole grains, dairy, and omega-3 fatty acids in your meals.

- Build a routine by having meals and snacks at the same time every day.

- Avoid skipping meals as it can result in lowering your blood sugar level.

- Stay away from junk and processed food.

- Take healthy foods such as fruits and nuts as quick snacks.

- Take advice from your doctor to include multivitamins and mineral supplements regularly if you are a picky eater or suffer from nutrient deficiencies.

- Go through all ingredient labels on food wrapping to avoid foods with artificial additives and high sugar content.

- Shop around those sections of a grocery store that hold minimally processed foods.

## Exercise Regularly

You already know how ADHD can make it quite challenging to concentrate on your work, finish tasks, and regulate your emotions. Research suggests that maintaining an active lifestyle that involves regular exercise and fitness sessions can improve your ability to think—it also calms down ADHD symptoms.

Regular exercise makes you more physically active and stimulates the brain cells indirectly. It also improves attention in people with ADHD by keeping a positive flow of emotions.

A few recent studies[20] have established that after spending 30 minutes in exercise, ADHD teens could comprehend and put together their thoughts in a better way.

Exercise helps release neurotransmitters (chemicals) in your body. These include dopamine and serotonin, which help with thinking clearly, paying attention to tasks, and staying

---

[20] https://www.ncbi.nlm.nih.gov/pmc/articles/PMC6945516/

calm in stressful situations. Those diagnosed with ADHD usually have low dopamine levels in their brain than those who don't have ADHD.

Fitness also has many other benefits for teens with ADHD:

- Eases anxiety

- Alleviates chronic stress

- Enhances your working memory

- Improves your impulse control

- Manages compulsive behavior

- It boosts the levels of brain-derived neurotrophic factor—a protein engaged in memory and learning. Since those with ADHD have lower levels of this protein, exercising regularly improves its levels, consequently helping with their condition.

- It strengthens your overall executive functions, including the ability to plan things, organize tasks and remember details pertinent to a task/activity.[21]

Because of these reasons, it is wise to incorporate physical activity into your routine.

Here's what you should do:

### *Play Any Sport You Enjoy*

Exercising does not mean you need to run on a treadmill for an hour or hit the gym daily. It means you need to engage in a rigorous physical activity that raises your heartbeat, pushes your muscles to work out, and energizes your body.

You can make this new shift enjoyable by playing any sport you enjoy. It could be basketball, baseball, badminton, swimming, or anything else. You could even dedicate one day of the week to each sport you play if you are involved in many sporting activities. For example, you can spend Mondays swimming, Tuesdays on football, Wednesdays on basketball, etc.

---

[21] https://wb.md/3JjEf86

Tag in a friend or two, or even a big group to amp up the fun. If you stick to the practice for a couple of weeks, you will see how enjoyable it becomes for you and how it helps with your ADHD.

Parents with ADHD teens should encourage their teenagers to play sports. If you have to, tend to the duty of dropping them off at playgrounds and then picking them up later. You could also play their favorite sport with them. It would make the experience more fun for them and give you better bonding time with your kids.

## *Run Around the Block*

You could also go for a run, jog, or brisk walk around the block. Pick any time of the day when you can spare some time and energize yourself with a good run.

During COVID-19, many walk and jog groups emerged as people felt the need to socialize due to the lockdown situation. You could locate any such group made up of kids your age. Perhaps you could create a walking/jogging/running group with friends and peers from school. Or you could even make one group for your family and relatives. All your loved ones could go for a nice, brisk walk together.

Whatever way you choose to do it—solo or in a group—ensure you stick to the practice for the long haul because that's the only way it would yield powerful, lasting results.

## *Do Some Stretches and Aerobics*

In addition, you could do some stretches and aerobics in the house, park, garden, or even in an exercise studio. If you enjoy yoga, Pilates, kickboxing, or even working out in the gym, do so.

Cycling is a great workout and activity for many people. If it is something you enjoy, try it out. You could rent a bicycle, borrow one from a friend, or even purchase one. Cycle around the block in the evening, and see how good it feels.

The idea is to work out and break a sweat. As long as you do that, the medium does not matter all that much. d

## *Start Small*

When it comes to working out, many of us get carried away with our enthusiasm initially. We are excited to try out something new, and the excitement makes us work out for even an hour at the start. However, that adrenaline rush soon fades away. That's when reality kicks in.

When that happens, many of us find ourselves quitting the practice halfway through. Perhaps this scenario resonates with you. Maybe you tried doing an activity for some time and then gave up.

Do you want that to happen to you this time? You really want to get a better grip on ADHD symptoms and live a happier, healthier life. To do that right, take things the 'slow and gradual' way this time around.

Instead of doing any physical activity for a longer period, start small. Begin with just 5 to 10, or a maximum of 15 minutes of any activity you choose to engage in. This is a great hack for building long-lasting habits that truly stick around for good. We easily lose our momentum when we have to do things outside our comfort zone. However, when we engage in the same tasks for small bits of time, we slowly settle into them. Once we gradually ease into the practice, we build it into a habit.

As soon as you build a habit of something, it shifts to your autopilot mode, which is when the magic truly begins to happen: you get the hang of the habit, you feel a natural inclination to do it, and you engage in it without thinking much.

This is what you need to achieve with your habit of regularly doing any physical activity. You should feel the urge to exercise and work out daily, and that happens best when you do it for small durations at the start.

Begin with just 5 to 10 minutes, and do it once or twice a day. For example, if you decide to cycle, go for a round of 5 or 10 minutes. Make sure to pick a time when you have nothing pressing to tend to or do. It will be easier to focus on physical activity when you have no urgent task to attend to. Once you have worked at it for about 3 weeks, you can increase the duration to 15 minutes. Stick to the 15-minute schedule for another 2 weeks, then stretch it to 20 or 25 minutes.

That's how you slowly build the habit of working out and make it a permanent activity in your life.

For parents of teens with ADHD reading this, please talk to your kids about this approach, and give them the support they need to practice it.

## *Get Enough Shuteye*

One of the most common concerns for teens with ADHD is getting adequate sleep because restlessness worsens ADHD symptoms. Research proves that an extra half-hour of good quality sleep[22] can help with agitation and impulsiveness.

Daytime sleepiness tends to have serious repercussions on work and school. It happens because you did not get enough shuteye at night. Struggling with ADHD means sleep deprivation will make you irritable, tired, grumpy, and restless. Plus, you will have a tough time focusing on your lectures at school, college, or your shift at work.

These symptoms are easy to mistake for grumpiness or a mood disorder. What we often ignore is the root cause of an issue. If you are constantly feeling droopy and grumpy during the day, it is time to fix your sleep routine.

---

[22]     https://www.webmd.com/sleep-disorders/ss/slideshow-sleep-disorders-overview

Here is how you can start fixing your sleep routine.

## Have a Consistent Bedtime Routine

Have a consistent and soothing bedtime[23] routine. You need to sleep for 7 to 9 hours at night. Set a fixed sleep time and wake-up time, making sure it gives you 7 to 9 hours of nighttime sleep.

Ensure to hit the bed at the exact time every night. You may keep tossing and turning in the bed during the first few days, and it is okay. When this happens, just stay put and don't use your phone. In a couple of weeks, you will adjust to the new routine and start sleeping well.

## Maintain a Comfortable Sleeping Environment

Keep the bedroom quiet and cold, or even slightly warm if that's the temperature you prefer. Make it sleep-friendly by turning off the lights. Turn on the fan if needed. Make different adjustments to your bedroom to ensure a comfortable sleeping environment that helps you initiate sleep easily. Also, check if the mattress and pillow are comfortable enough.

---

[23] https://www.webmd.com/parenting/childs-bedtime

## Have a Winding Down Ritual

Stick to a relaxing winding-down ritual such as taking a bath before bed, dedicating 15-minutes to reading, or inscribing in a journal. Try any mind-calming exercise, such as counting down from 100 to 1.

Do not allow any pets on the bed. They may stretch or alter body positions, waking you up during your sleep.

Stick to these guidelines, and do your best to get to bed at your bedtime religiously. Soon, you will adjust to the new sleep routine and start to sleep well.

# Conclusion

I am so thankful to you for taking the time to read this book and being courageous enough to seek a solution to ADHD. You are amazing; always believe that.

Having ADHD does not lower your potential. It only makes you human. If you religiously stick to the guidelines in this book, I am positive you will start seeing magical effects soon and move on to living a very meaningful life.

PS: I'd like your feedback. If you are happy with this book, please leave a review on Amazon.

Please leave a review for this book on Amazon by visiting the page below:

https://amzn.to/2VMR5qr

Printed in Great Britain
by Amazon

85792988R00047